Neil Curry

SOME LETTERS
NEVER SENT

ENITHARMON PRESS

First published in 2014
by Enitharmon Press
10 Bury Place
London WC1A 2JL

www.enitharmon.co.uk

Distributed in the UK by
Central Books
99 Wallis Road
London E9 5LN

Distributed in the USA and Canada
by Dufour Editions Inc.
PO Box 7, Chester Springs
PA 19425, USA

ISBN: 978-1-907587-76-4

Enitharmon Press gratefully acknowledges the financial support of
Arts Council England, through Grants for the Arts.

British Library Cataloguing-in-Publication Data.
A catalogue record for this book is available
from the British Library.

Designed in Albertina by Libanus Press
and printed in England by
SRP

For Natasha and Victoria

ACKNOWLEDGEMENTS

Some of these poems first appeared in the following publications:

Bow-Wow Shop, The Dark Mountain, English, Illuminations, Killing the Angel, London Magazine, Poetry Ireland, The Reader, The Richard Jefferies Society Journal, Scintilla, Temenos Academy Review, Trespass Magazine.

My thanks also go to The Blue Mountain Center and to The Ucross Foundation.

'An odd thought strikes me: we shall receive
no letters in the grave.'

SAMUEL JOHNSON

CONTENTS

IN PRAISE OF LETTERS

February 1801. Dove Cottage.
Wordsworth is opening his post

with the butter knife.
There is a letter from Charles Lamb.

He is not coming. He has
turned down their invitation.

> *'Separate from the pleasure*
> *of your company, I don't much care*
> *if I never see a mountain in my life.'*

he writes.

Listen, and you can
still hear
the silence
that followed
that Wordsworthian
sniff.

As you may hear too the squeals
and meows when Cassandra Austen
reads yet another catty missive from her sister, Jane:

> *'She appeared exactly as she did*
> *in September, with the same broad face,*
> *diamond bandeau, white shoes,*
> *pink husband, and fat neck.'*

I had this notion once
that I would buy a *Compendium of Letters,*

(there's bound to be one in Oxfam)
cut them up, and post them to myself,
one by one, so that every day
among the offers of cut-price car insurance
there'd be something akin to Johnson's
put-down of Lord Chesterfield.

What better way to begin the morning?
There would be sad ones:
Lowell to Elizabeth Bishop,
reminding her how once she'd said:

> 'When you come to write my epitaph,
> you must say I was the loneliest
> person who ever lived.'

And there'd be those grim ones from the Front:

> ' . . . their faces grey and disfigured; dark
> stains of blood soaking through their torn
> garments, all hope and merriment
> snuffed out forever.'

But there would
be delightful ones too:
from Coleridge
and Cowper,
not to mention Keats.

These cut-ups would be in print of course,
so never the same as something
hand-written coming through the door.

We want to be able to say:
'*This is the paper*
her hand rested on.
These are the marks that her pen made.'

Love-letters – a case in point –
need to be sealed with a lipstick kiss.

I had one so precious to me once
I folded it into a tiny square
and kept it inside my wallet,
but took it out,
read it
and re-read it so often
that it fell to bits.

The actual words
have escaped me,
but I do recall –
like Gael Turnbull (that lovely man)
telling me of a book he thought I ought to read,
and finding that although he had forgotten
not only the title, the name of the author
and every single thing about it,
he still knew for sure that:

> '*reading it had been*
> *an intensely pleasurable experience.*'

TO: MR RICHARD JEFFERIES, COATE FARM, NR. SWINDON

I was in Eagle Lake, one of those
Quiet little towns in Upper New York State –
One Main Street and a white clapboard church –
Rummaging about in its Used Book Store,
When I came across a copy of your *Bevis*.
So alien there; so very English,
It cried out to be liberated
And brought back home.

           Starting to read it
Somewhere over the Atlantic, somewhere
Off Greenland, I found myself remembering
The exact shelf in the School Library
I'd first found it on – near those leather-bound books
Which you only had to touch and they'd leave
Your fingers stained bright orange and smelling
Of cat-piss.

           I would have been eleven.
Bevis. A story of the boyhood I wished
I was having: the best friend; the fields
And woods you played in; sunshine; adventures;
And your 'governor' teaching you to swim
In the river.

           Recently though, I've read
That we had more in common than I knew:
You, solitary, moody; your family
Short of money; the usual bickering
And nastiness; your mother despising,
And teaching you to despise, your father.

By twelve though, I have to confess
I'd swapped allegiance to Arthur Ransome,
To *Swallows and Amazons* and to
My all-time favourite, *Great Northern?*

The great northern diver. Years had gone by
With precious little chance of me seeing one,
Yet only hours after buying *Bevis*
I had heard . . .
                  'What *is* that?'
                             'It's the loons,'
Said Ben, 'out there on the lake.'

                          I listened
To that haunted wail, as if they were
Giving voice to something that had long been
Unsettling their own ghosts. And it went on.

TO: TIMOTHY THE TORTOISE, 'THE WAKES', SELBORNE, HAMPSHIRE

No end of letters came for Mr White,
Which is why this one, Timothy, is aimed
At you, somewhere, I hope, in his garden,
Under the broad beans perhaps, or if you're
Really lucky and nobody's noticed as yet,
Happily chomping away among the strawberry beds.

He'd grown very fond of you, you know,
And as autumn came and the days darkened,
He'd watch out for where you went burrowing
Down into the warmth of the compost heap,
Safely stowing your legs in under your own self's roof,
Ready for what he unkindly called your 'joyless stupor'.

Joyless? I wonder what he thought you
Would be missing out on: chilblains, chapped hands, ice
And snow? Mr W. himself awoke
One morning to find the water frozen
Solid in his bedside decanter. When spring came though
He'd be eager to greet you, announcing in his Journal:

'Timothy did come forth and march about.'
Hibernation was a constant puzzle
To him. Swallows? Africa? Surely not.
At times you caught the rougher end of this
Spirit of Enquiry. Being dunked into a pail
Of water to see if you could swim must have been nasty.

But for the most part, Timothy, you had
An easy life. No one harnessed you up
To pull a plough, or ever expected
You to bark, grow wool, lay eggs, or catch mice.

And as for your master – even at the risk of death
From cholera, typhoid, smallpox, the ague, or mumps,

I would gladly swap lives with him; take on his worries:
Was it *true* that bats would fly down people's
Chimneys to gnaw at the bacon hanging
In their kitchens? Naturalist-cum-parson-
cum-poet, yes, I think I could manage that. I'd preach
The Wisdom of God as manifest in His Creation.

Consider the divine œconomy
shown in that most lowly of amphibians
the frog: aquatic first, it sinuates
the tail of a fish; but, when his legs appear,
that same appendage, deemed useless now, drops off
and the creature doth betake itself to land.

Sorry, I got carried away a bit then. Before
You toddle off though to snooze in the forest
Of asparagus, let me echo Gilbert's
Closing words to his friend Mr Pennant
And assure you that every incident
Which occasions a renewal of our correspondence
Will ever be pleasing and agreeable to me.

TO: EDMUND SANDARS, C/O OUP (OR TRY RSPB)

Thanks to your *Bird Book for the Pocket*, I could
By the age of nine or ten, identify
Most of the birds of Britain – well,
As long as they were facing to the left that is.

Coming across it again yesterday quite
By chance – it had slipped down behind *Tristram Shandy*
And a volume of Cowper's *Letters* – I'd forgotten
Just how truly bizarre some

Of your illustrations are. Your dabchick for one
Looks more like a toad than a bird. In truth
Precious few would appear to have much propensity
For flight – what with their gormless grins

And L.S. Lowry legs. But your entries
Under *Manners* are a delight. How else
Could I have guessed that a green woodpecker can hop
Backwards; that bearded tits hate the wind;

That snipe tend to be lethargic, yet have
Ravenous appetites. But I shouldn't mock.
You meant so much to so many of us once.
(My copy is the seventh impression of a third edition.)

And times change. Seemingly you expected us
To hear a corncrake, the booming of bitterns,
Or the 'Little-bit-of-bread-and-no-cheeeeese'
Of the yellowhammer. Small chance of that now.

Every bit as sad though is the *rara avis* you
Yourself have become – *avis rarissima* one might say.
I've trawled your name through the internet and come up with
Nothing. No, not even on Wikipedia.

TO: N.C. C/O L'AUBERGE DE FRANCE, AVIGNON

I'd been clearing stuff out of my desk drawer
When I chanced on your diary. I say *yours,*

But really it's that of someone with whom
I shared – years ago, decades in fact –
More than just a name. Now the handwriting

Doesn't even look that familiar.
Nineteen you must have been when you bought it.
It's good quality – hardback – with the price

Inside it still – 325 old francs.
So not cheap. It was what you took with you
When you set out to hitch to Andorra

And was just about the bulkiest thing
You had in your duffle bag – that and the tins
Of cigarettes – *Markovitch Black and White* –

You smoked then. At least you made it as far south
As Avignon. And Avignon certainly
Filled up a few pages, didn't it? Not

That I'd ever betray your confidence
On that score. You have my word, I promise.
But then you don't. And that's the pity of it.

I read these words of yours, but you – you
Will never read a single one of mine.
It's unfair, and I don't like to think

Of you left behind there in the past.
It feels as though we had abandoned you.

Do you remember it ever raining
When we were together, Lucienne? I can't.
It was beginning to feel like the end
Of autumn though, that October evening

When we sat for the last time together
On what had always been our favourite
Bench, just inside the edge of the Forest.
Later you wrote to me to say how cold

It was getting there. 'Le froid, comme une seconde
Sagesse, saurait faire entendre raison
Même aux plus imprudents.' A Bretonne,
And stubborn, 'Têtue comme une Bretonne,'

As you used to warn me; you would insist
On correcting my French until I'd got it
Right. We were very young, very happy,
And very much in love. Long afternoon

Walks we took together through the Forest,
Or in the Palace Gardens, where we would
Flick those little aluminium
One franc pieces into the lake, and watch

For the giant carp to come rising up,
Half-swallow them, then spit them out again.
Most Saturday nights meant *L'Ermitage* for us,
The cinema next to the Café Richelieu.

But some weekends we got away
To Paris, and I still have that drawing
One of the quick-fire artists made of you
In the Place du Tertre. He'd caught the line

Of your cooky cheeks to perfection.
We went to Longchamps once – I think we won.
And once out to see the *son et lumière*
At Versailles, where the colours blew our minds.

But then that drear October evening came,
As it had to, and I can remember
The warmth of the yellow and russet jacket
You were wearing. But not, no, not

How we ever managed to decide which
Of all our kisses that night was to be
The very last. No. I wonder, Cauchemar,
My love, if you can remember. I can't.

TO: ΚΥΡΙΟΣ EURIPIDES, ON THE ISLAND OF SALAMIS

I've heard you used to like to sit and write
At the mouth of a small cave, looking out
Over the Aegean. Well, who wouldn't,
What with that sky, the sea, the solitude;
And a little bread and cheese perhaps, and some
Wine cooling in the shade?

                          I am sitting
On the beach at Aldingham. Here the sea
And the sky are the same gun-metal grey.
A wind's getting up, and I'm beginning to wish
I'd brought my gloves.

                        The way the trees
Are swaying further down the coast puts me
In mind of some lines of yours from *The Bacchae*.
How *did* you manage that? Finding an image,
A simile, to describe – of all things –
A circle?

               Dionysus is bending
A tall pine tree: *Down, down to the green earth,*
Bending it like a bow, like a circle,
Like – and then you added – *like when you take*
A peg and line and trace a wheel rim
Out upon the ground. So simple, yet so
Perfect.

               I'm sure I'd never have the nerve
To tell you that though, were we ever
To meet up in Hades; I'd be far too
Shame-faced, having, as it were, 'translated'
Your plays, knowing next to nothing of the
Language you wrote them in.

But I couldn't stand
The way that you, and others, had been *Classic-ised*.
It was that beggar's *bollocks* they threatened
To rip off, not his *vital organs*.
And it took me weeks to convince some don
Moonlighting at CUP that you
Had a sense of humour.

By the by, did you know
That waves are not the solid body
Of moving water they look to be,
But a 'pattern of energy' moulding the water
It's passing through? No, no more did I.
All the same I never tire of watching
The rhythms they build up as they surge
And break – that rush of sibilance, then
The gravelled undertow.

And the sea
Plays such a part in what you wrote.
I remember Poseidon's bullish waves
Swelling, boiling, crashing when they destroyed
Hippolytus.

But did it rile you
That you so rarely won the prizes? But then
Did it surprise you? To stage the bloody
Aftermath of the Trojan war, with all
The atrocities committed by the Greeks
Was one thing, but to show it so soon
After your troops had done the selfsame thing
To the people of Melos was asking
For trouble. There must have been politicians
Wriggling about on their fat bums that day.

In my copy of *The Trojan Women*
There's a cutting from *The Times*: a junta
Of 60s' colonels in Athens had declared
Your plays '*subversive of society,*
Of the King and of religion,' and they
Banned them.

You'd died in 406 BC,
Yet were still subversive. What more need one say?

I see the tide's on the turn, coming in
With those little skittering runs that get
The oystercatchers so jittery. I felt
Some spots of rain then, I think. High time
I packed all this away and headed home. You don't
Mind if we just leave it at that, do you?

TO: MS ANGELA CARTER, THE BERKELEY CAFÉ, BRISTOL

It's not there now, but then no more are you.
Were this to find you anywhere though, Ange,
I would like to think it was The Berkeley,
After the hours we spent together there.

Mature students we were meant to be,
Not that anyone would have guessed
From our ritual morning challenges:
You: Waiter, waiter, there's a fly in my soup.

Me: Give in. *You*: Yes, Sir, it's trouser soup.
And then you'd laugh, that breathless laugh of yours
That sounded like a puppy choking.
The 'children' seemed almost afraid of you,

Especially in seminars. You had read,
It seemed, nearly every Russian novel
There was – surreptitiously though, as you
Once confessed, when you were the court reporter,

Bored beyond belief, for some local paper,
Clapham, was it? At times you could be
So cutting. Do you recall that pale,
Flat-chested girl who read Old Norse and wore

Those long silver necklaces? You called her
The Muse in Chains. And you got no better.
Years later, after a reading you'd given
In Lancaster, a little old lady

Asked you where you got your ideas from.
'I make 'em up,' you growled at her. 'It's my
Fucking job.' There was no need for that.
But back in our busy Berkeley days

My *Bacchae* had been shown on television
And you were writing your *Shadow Dance*
That students are writing dissertations
On today. Dissertations? That was another of our

Contests. I remember winning one with
'Some Studies in the Rhetorical Use
Of the Full Stop in Johnson's *Rasselas*.'
Only to hear some visiting speaker

Refer next day to a Johnsonian *The*.
That had us both snorting behind our fists.
Footnotes? Well, there was that grey, bedraggled
Woman who came and wiped our tables down

With her wet dishcloth. You called her (we'd been
Reading Swift) *The Struldbrug*. I know she's in there
Somewhere. And one morning you said you'd been
Dribbling syrup over your porridge

In patterns 'like ecclesiastical
Embroidery.' We smoked so much those days
The air would get to be a dishcloth grey
And almost about as thick as porridge.

Over the road – it seems ironic now –
Was the Wills Tower and Library, built by
W.D. and H.O. out of their
Profits from the stuff that would account for you.

We had been warned. A clown in one of Ben
(The other Jonson's) plays attacked the weed:
'Who knows,' he said, 'but that the alligator
Hath not pissed thereon?' Bloody alligators.

TO: DR BASIL COTTLE, DEPT OF ENGLISH, THE UNIVERSITY, BRISTOL

Arthur Basil Cottle. It was only seeing
   Your obituary made me remember
The *Arthur*, which, as you once confided to me,
   You thought, 'Too fluffy for everyday use.'
Preferring (who knows why?) to be known as *Basil*.
   No one though was ever more deserving
Of those initials: *ABC*.

Middle English
   You taught us – Monday mornings 9 a.m. –
Reading *Sir Gawain* to us until I felt like
   Hugging myself to keep warm, hearing of those
Winter scenes: '*When Þe colde cler water was from Þe cloudez*
   Schadden and fres er it falle myzht
To Þe fale erÞe.' Then sitting up straight again
   When, '*he herde a little dyn at his dor.*'
What could it be? You paused. Yes, '*hit waÞ Þe laidi,*
   Loflyest to be holde.'

Lover of old
Poems, old churches, and all things Welsh, in fact
   Of everything that ever was or is,
I remember one teatime in our kitchen,
   Natasha on your knee, chewing at the end
Of your tie, and you happened to observe
   That the blue and white of our milk jug
Were not only the colours of the national flag
   Of Greece, but also those of Ipswich Town
Football Club.

     Naturally enough, when they were looking
   For lateral thinkers, the War Office

Posted you to Bletchley Park to help to solve
    The Enigma Code. The *Albanian*
Grammar you compiled there must have helped in some way
    I suppose.

                    Unworldly, yet the kindliest
Of men; when Susie Tucker, herself a brilliant
    Linguist, had that stroke and lost
The power of speech, there you were at her hospital
    Bedside, emptying out the letters
Of your Scrabble set so that she could talk to you.
    Words of course were always your chief delight.
Names too, and my copy of your *Dictionary*
    Of English Surnames has a well-thumbed look.
Just a pity that *Curry* isn't in it.
    Etym. Dub., as you explained. But *Raper* is.
'An unfortunate name, but which, as you know,'
    (Of course I didn't) 'means no more than
Rope-Maker.' Then you found in the London Phone Book
    A Mr Raper living at 11
Sabine Row. A gift too good to miss. There he is now,
    Made briefly famous on page 234.
I do wish though that I could have shared with you
    That in the *British Journal of Urology*
There was once an article on *Incontinence*
    Co-authored by Messrs. Weedon and Splatt.

TO: SIR JOHN BARROW, DRAGLEY BECK, ULVERSTON

1. **Barrow:** (a) a large mound of earth or stones
                    placed over a burial site
           (b) a pig that has been castrated before
                    reaching sexual maturity
2. **Barrow:**   Sir John (1764–1846), Second Secretary
                    to the Admiralty

Anyone travelling here by train
from the south, and looking out
as it crosses the viaduct,
sees the great sweep
of Morecambe Bay:

redshank and dunlin
fossicking out on the mudflats,
herons hunched in the shallows,

then, on the right,
just after those cottages
at Next Ness,
there is your '*Monument*',

that hundred-foot high
pepper-pot replica
of the Eddystone Lighthouse
up on the top of Hoad Hill,

'The Hoad monument',
as we call it these days,
having just about forgotten you,
the way you forgot about Ulverston.

Today, Ulverston is a
contented, perhaps a little

inward-looking town.
I've heard tourists call it quaint:
its cobbled Market Street,
a bakers, two butchers,
two hardware stores,
and even, praise be,
a bookshop;
and not so very long ago
we had a haberdashery
and a café
that closed for lunch.

But back in your time
it was a busy little port,
where men really did make rope
in the Rope Walk.
Anchors were cast in the foundry;
ships built
and launched off Greenodd.

But all this was
so much small change
for you. You wanted
city-life. You wanted
power and (let's not mince words)
you wanted fame.
You wanted to be known
as the man who filled in
those last little gaps in the Atlas:
the course of the Niger, and
of course, your real obsession:
the North-West Passage.

From behind the redoubt
of your desk
you despatched them:
team after team
of eager young men –
into the Sahara,
where, if they weren't cut down
by the Tauregs,
yellow fever killed them off.

And you were, oh so
contemptuous of their failure.

They failed you in the Arctic too,
'Amid all its brilliancy,'
Ross wrote, 'this land of ice
and snow is a heart-sinking
dreary and monotonous waste,
so cheerless, cold and still
one's very mind is paralysed.'

Barrow Strait, Cape Barrow,
Barrow Sound, your cartographers
did their best to placate you,
but died in doing so:
starvation, or scurvy,
or simply the cold.

No one ever knew
what befell Franklin's men,
but you, you managed
to keep on going into your 80s
and when you retired

your colleagues in the Admiralty
gave you that selfsame desk
as a leaving present.

Ever the consummate bureaucrat,
you failed to see the joke.

You know,
a man by the name of
Adolf Eichmann
was hanged for a lifetime's work
not that dissimilar from your own.

But then
we are all sons of Cain, I suppose.
We all of us have heritage.

TO: MRS ANNA MARIA SMART C/O *THE READING MERCURY*, READING, BERKSHIRE

I have sat and listened to feminists
Going on and on about how women
Were held back in the eighteenth century.

They hadn't met you though, had they, Anna?
I'd like to see what could have held you back,
Leastways, once you'd got shot of your husband.

Kit must, I grant you, have been a trial:
The bright young Cambridge don turned drag-artiste;
The alcoholic who got religion.

He prayed so loud once in St James's Park
That he 'routed all the company'
Until the watchmen came and beat him up.

It was all very embarrassing. And you?
As your younger daughter nicely put it:
'Queen Bess herself was not more absolute.'

You had him locked away in a madhouse,
And went off to Dublin with the sole rights
To Dr James's famous 'Fever Powder'.

Nature or nurture? Where did you get that
Business acumen? John Newbery
My guess would be – bookseller, stepfather,

Entrepreneur, and advertising man
Of genius. *Jack Whirler* they called him.
Did he strike a deal with Dr Potter?

The next we hear of you, you're Managing
Editor of *The Reading Mercury*,
But with a great dislike of anything

Relating to literature. '. . . though married'
This from your daughter again, 'to an author,
Or perhaps from that very circumstance.'

And Christopher? Well, many (Gray included)
Thought he was dead. But not so. He'd dried out;
Tended a small garden; grew pinks,

And had acquired (who knows how?) a cat
By the name of Jeoffry, who would spraggle
Upon waggle at the word of command.

His own Magnificat. In his nature
Christopher quested for beauty, but God,
'God,' he said. 'hath sent me to sea for pearls.'

It must really piss you off to know that,
Especially since we owe it all to you,
Mrs Smart. Yes, all of it, we owe to you.

TO: MISS EMILY DICKINSON, THE HOMESTEAD.
AMHERST

That really was a bit of a whopper
You told when you said your poems were your
Letter to the World that never wrote to you.

The mailman must have come knocking at your door
Day in day out. Not that you ever went
To open it of course. No. Visitors

Talked of hallowed things aloud and embarrassed
Your dog; whereas letters were, 'The Mind alone,
Without corporeal Friend.' Reclusive?

Well, you once declared that for several years
Your closest companion had been your Lexicon.
And I can understand that, as it was you

Who showed us the way single words
May have poetry enough within themselves
To elbow out whole sentences. And here

I am thinking of *dimity* and *heft* and *plush*.
You had to make do with *Noah Webster*,
Which was a pity. If you'd been in time

For the OED to come along, what
Wouldn't you have shown us then! In England
Your contemporaries had Samuel Johnson,

A 'harmless drudge' according to his own
Definition, but a fine poet too.
He had his off-moments though: **THIN**: *not thick.*

THICK: *not thin.* Even so Browning read him
Right through, I believe, and I can see why.
Take **SEAL**, for example: *in make and growth*

Not unlike a pig, ugly-faced, and footed
Like a moldwarp. Or TARANTULA:
An insect whose bite is only cured

By music. And it's to Johnson I owe
The word **VATICIDE**, which means to murder
A poet. But he never got so lost

In lexicography as to forget
That while words may be the daughters of earth,
It's things which are the sons of heaven.

Did you have a favourite word? It's sound
I think decides it for me. *Oriflamme*
I have in a poem somewhere, but this

I suspect, is the last chance I'm going to get
To work in *cochineal*, or *libellule*,
That gorgeous word the French have for a dragon-fly.

TO: DR PETER MARK ROGET, THE PORTICO LIBRARY, MANCHESTER

I hardly dare to get my chess set down;
Not now, not since I learnt you'd found a way
To move a knight so that it lands on each
And every square, but never the same square twice!

That kind of flaky challenge could prove
Even more addictive than Sudoku.
But, like those lists of words you made, such things
Provided your own *stay against confusion*.
And what confusion.
                           Madness didn't just
Run in you family, did it? No, it
Careered, scampered, galloped, sprinted, sped,
And *made haste.*

              And then there were those suicides:
The uncle who cut his throat, and splattered
You all over with his blood as he died.

No wonder you felt safer in a world
Of words. Words you could order, classify.

In the public world, as a physician,
Your aim was the erasing of disease:
Smallpox, cholera, typhoid and *the clap.*
But in Manchester? In 1804?
Small chance of that.
                           There look to be over
Two hundred entries under your one
Heading of *Uncleanliness.*

                                          So it must have been
A haven for you then, The Portico:
The cigar smoke, the armchairs, and the books.

'What do you read, my Lord?'
                                          Words, words, words.

It is ironic though the way your name
Has become synonymous with synonyms
When you didn't believe in them.
                                          Some shades, yes,
Some affiliations, convergencies.
For a girl may be good-looking, yet not
Gorgeous, pretty, cute, or even *beautiful.*
And while some summer days are beautiful,
None are ever cute.
                               Every word unique
In itself, distinct.

                               What you offered was
A helping hand to all those *painfully*
Struggling with the difficulties
Of Composition.
                               'I just can't put it
Into words.'

                    Plath once confessed to being
A 'Roget's strumpet' and I myself wore
My first copy out completely.
                                     We really should
Be more grateful to you.

                        At least
They've put a plaque up to you now
Outside The Portico, and you'll be pleased to know
That men of letters often meet there still,
One being my good friend Grevel Lindop,
Poet, scholar, salsa-dancer
And Thomas De Quincey fan.
                                    We're lunching there
Next Tuesday week, and we'll drink a toast to you.
Join us, why don't you, in spirit at least.

TO: THE VENERABLE BEDE, MONKWEARMOUTH, JARROW

I've always liked that story of the monk
Carving your tombstone and being at a loss
For words, well for an adjective at least,

To put in front of *bones* – so he left a gap
And overnight an angel came and filled it in
With *venerabilis* – a name (it does now

Seem to be your name) that's really stuck.
There's something sort of *mildewed* though
About Venerable; it makes me think

Of *verdigris*, as if your Benedictine robe
Weren't always quite as fresh as it might have been,
And makes you seem perpetually old,

Which of course you weren't. Another story
Has it you were the little lad 'nourished and taught'
By Ceolfrith, you and he the only survivors

When the Third Rider – plague – trampled down Jarrow.
Frightening for a child it must have been: those bulbos
Big as apples, the retching and the deadly

Ring o' roses before the skin turned black.
Thanks be your own death was more gentle.
As you said: having lived without shame

You could die without fear. But managing
To hold on until you'd finished translating *John*,
That was a nice touch – those closing words of his:

'I suppose that even the world itself
Could not contain the books that should be written.'
How many you yourself had written is something

I suppose we will never know. Alone
In your cell with your lampblack ink, and pens,
Recounting the exploits of the saints,

Their voyages, their miracles and derring-do,
There were times you doubted whether what you'd done
Had been enough, you who'd never ventured

Further than Lindisfarne, and that only once,
While so many of your friends had made their way
To Rome and back. But you were the maker. Without

You, we would never have known of the otters
That came running to dry Saint Cuthbert's feet
With their fur after he'd been praying in the sea;

Or of Edwin's thane likening our lives
To the flight of a sparrow – coming in from
A howling winter's storm, into the light

And warmth of the mead hall, where great lords
Sat feasting, then straightway out into the storm again;
Or of the poet Cædmon who fled

From the song only to be found by the Singer.
Only books? Bede, hinny, you showed us miracles
Can flare out from so little as the turning of a page.

TO: JOB IN THE LAND OF UZ

You must, as they say, have been thunderstruck
When His voice came at you out of the whirlwind,
So totally OTT: all that bombast
And brou-ha-ha, and all of it beside the point.

'Have you walked through the depths of the ocean?'
He wanted to know. 'Will the unicorn
Harrow the fields behind you? And the hawk,
Does it soar up and spread its wings at your command?'

Then sillier still. 'Tell me, canst thou catch
The serpent, Leviathan, with an hook,
And will he then speak soft words to you?'
Now, in my experience, when someone rants on

This way, then more often than not, there is
Something they are trying to avoid.
And in your case, what you were never told,
Is that all your troubles boiled down to a bet.

Satan just happened to drop in on the
High Court of Heaven one day, and God said,
'Where have you been?' 'Oh, wandering here and there
On earth,' said Satan, flicking back his ponytail

And hitching up his jeans. 'Looking around.'
'And did you see Job?' 'Job? Sure I saw Job.
He's doing very nicely, thank you.
Ten great kids he's got, and all those donkeys and slaves,

Oxen and sheep. And at least three thousand
Camels. You've been good to him. No wonder
He says he loves you. But if I were to . . .'
Then came the bet. 'You'd hear him curse you to your face.'

God paused a moment to think it over.
With your reputation, he couldn't lose.
He took the bet. 'All right, do whatever
You want, but on one condition: you don't kill him.'

And so, before you knew it, you were childless,
Homeless, with not a camel to your name,
Squatting there alone among the ashes
On the city dump, cysts and pustules from head to foot,

Yes, and more than a suspicion of AIDS.
Man, even the lepers steered clear of you.
Not exactly above board, was it? Oh, you cursed.
'Cursèd be the day that I was born,' you began.

'My bowels boil within me and my skin
Blackens and peels. My bones are on fire.
I am brother to the wild jackal,
And a companion to owls.' Not once though did you think

To curse God. 'Why me?' you wanted to know.
'Wherefore do the wicked live and grow old,
Yea and prosper?' But you see that's what they
Dared not tell you, or their wager would have been void.

So you still want to know? It's that old scene;
We've all played it. 'Do you love me? No, really?
How much do you love me? But what if I . . . ?
Or putting it another way, the question is:

Is totally undeserved punishment
A moral necessity in order
To have a world in which a completely
Selfless love is at least a possibility?

Now I don't know what your lawyers would have
Made of this, Job, but the words *Crimes Against
Humanity* keep running through my mind,
And I cannot manage to shake them off.

TO: MRS MARGARET FELL, SWARTHMOOR HALL, ULVERSTON

Were it not for the plaque by the gate
There'd be no way of knowing
This tussocky bit of land up on Birkrigg
Had ever been a graveyard,
Or that you yourself now lay buried here.

But were you to pass this way again
I think you'd find it looking
Much the same, though Benson's peacocks would take you
Somewhat by surprise. The Hall
At Swarthmoor has undergone some changes,

Even so, you'd know it for your home,
And Morecambe Bay is still the same;
The sweep of the incoming tide still as fast
And the danger still the same
As the time it so nearly caught out George.

It was the simplest of ideas
He'd brought over with him:
That in each of us there is the Inner Light
Of Christ; but more dangerous
Than a rip tide, because, if true, there'd be

No need for priests, or 'steeple houses'.
And when he preached that doctrine
In St Mary's, Ulverston, the faithful, in their rage,
Kicked him damned near to death.
Mind you, he'd also told them they were,

'Liars, drunkards, whoremongers and thieves,'
Which hadn't helped his cause much.

Oh, and I forgot to tell you: Lancaster
Castle was still a jail
Until recently – one you knew too well.

Four years for refusing the Oath,
Four years of solitary
For George, and in a cell open to the worst
Of the weather – rain and snow.
The torments they put you through then seem light years

Away from today's white-haired gentlefolk
In their Meeting Houses, eyelids stilled, and smiling
Benignly, as though (I might be wrong of course)
A cup of tea and a custard cream
Were uppermost in their minds just now.

TO: MR ROBERT SUTTON, WORCESTER CATHEDRAL

Did you opt to be buried in your boots?
Well, were they the ones you wore when you walked
To Santiago, then I'm not surprised.
I've kept mine. But mine won't turn up again
After five hundred years the way yours did
When they were digging under the Great Tower
Of Worcester Cathedral. Experts picked and scraped
And brushed away the dirt, and there you were –
In your long woollen robe; your pilgrim's staff
And a cockleshell lying alongside you.

I can't claim to have walked the Camino
The way you did. I took the train through France
Down as far as Saint-Jean Pied de Port. You
Opened your front door one morning, set out
And walked every step of the way. Why though?
For my part, it was as if I were told to.
Were I to say a *voice*, you'd probably
Understand, whereas most people today
Would look so askance at me that I don't
Do it. Walking that far seems odd enough.

But you, six months it must have taken you
And that's a long time to have been away
From your family and your business. So
Were you sent? Was it a penance? Was it
Due to something Mrs Sutton
Had taken exception to? I'm sorry.
I shouldn't pry. It earned you several years
Remission from Purgatory though, didn't it?
We no longer believe in that. Instead
We create it, over and over again, down here

In ways you couldn't begin to imagine.
One thing I really do envy you
Is that you would have been 'surprised by joy'.
You didn't carry a guide book with you.
You hadn't read the travel supplements
Or seen the TV documentaries.
You didn't know what was coming around
The next corner let alone the next town.
I had seen it all before I saw it.
Sadly, you travelled without the benefit

Of *Gore-Tex*. I got soaked through even so
Crossing the Pyrenees, but when I reached
The Abbey of Roncevaux the monks there
Dried my clothes, ran a bath for me and balanced
A double brandy on the end of it.
Splendid men they are those Benedictines.
I walked alone; you'd have sought company
For safety's sake as much as anything.
I've read that there were cougars, bears and wolves
Along the road as well as bandits.

Aymery Picaud wrote that the people
Of Navarre were 'debauched, perfidious,
Drunken, ferocious and impolite.' What
I remember most about Navarre is a
White wine which was the colour of honey.
It's odd, don't you think, the memories we bring
Home with us? In Burgos I asked a lady
The way to the House of El Cid. 'No es
Una casa, es más una cosa,'
She said. What a sentence. I could have kissed her.

And the cathedral at Leon. So much
Stained glass it was like being inside
A fire opal. I wrote a poem
About it, sitting one quiet afternoon
In a field, eating dried apricots,
While stick insects crawled up and down
The blades of grass beside me. That was one
Of the good things of walking by myself.
But did you tell stories to each other
The way Chaucer's pilgrims did? You must have.

And did you stand at night in the doorway
Of your *refugio*, looking up at the pale
Arm of the Milky Way – pointing you westwards –
The road under the stars? Then you were there:
Santiago de Compostela. And like
Millions of others you would have reached up
To touch the Stem of Jesse Column
In the Portico de Gloria. You know
So many have done so since there are now five
Half-inch indentations in the marble!

Each of us, seemingly, has taken
Something away with him. But left something too:
The elation of a thing achieved; the shared
Experience. Have you noticed that I've not
Once mentioned Saint James? As I've said before,
It's hard to be sure whether the absence
Of his presence, or the presence of his
Absence is now the more telling. When I
Walked through the door of the *Hostal Suso*
And was given a glass of cold beer

A dish of olives, and with Vivaldi
Playing on the tape-deck I thought then
I must have died and was in Paradise.
They re-buried you, you'll be glad to know.
Well, they might have put your bones and all your
Other bits and pieces on display
In a museum somewhere. But you're still
In Worcester where you belong, where you can
Hear the anthems and the quiet prayers,
As is only right. You earned your repose.

TO: FATHER IGNACIO DE MADRID, EL MONASTERIO DE SANTA MARIA DEL PARRAL, SEGOVIA

That, Ignacio, my friend, was a moment
I will not forget: when you casually
Took down from its shelf a fat vellum tome
And putting it into my hands said that this,
This was Erasmus's own copy of the Works
Of Saint Jerome, and *Mira*, you said, 'Look'
Pointing to places where he'd crossed out –
Totally obliterated in fact –
Ideas he couldn't go along with.

One idea that I myself find it hard
To go along with is that it's now
Sixty-eight years since you first became
A member of this Order. You were then
Seventeen. Forgive me, but that word
Obliterated comes to mind again.
Damn it though (sorry) you look well enough
On it – except for the state of your teeth;
But then your food is truly awful.

Meeting you has made me hope that there just might
Be an after-life – some sort of recompense.
But what? There would surely be some people
Even you wouldn't really want to see,
And how long do you think any of us
Could tolerate having to have all
Our wishes met? And a 'wearisome
Eternity of warbled hymns' was something
Even Milton couldn't bear to think of.

Maybe then, Ignacio, you have it here
Already: the cool of the cloisters,
A clear Castilian sky, pinks and roses,
The fountains and the water-gardens,
And handling books Erasmus himself once held.

TO: MR WILLIAM TYNDALE, VILVORDE CASTLE, BELGIUM

In the beginning was the Word,
But the words, variously, were in Latin,
Greek and Hebrew, not to mention Aramaic,
And that, as you saw it, was the problem.

Why, you wanted to know, should not
The husbandman, who driveth his plough, sing
Them out loud in the fields, or the weaver
Warble them as he works at his shuttle?

As I write this to you in late
September 2010, I wonder
How often next year it'll be acknowledged
That great swathes of the Authorized Version

Had been cribbed directly from you.
In one of his more frosty seasons Thomas More
Described your work as 'the most pestiferous
And pernicious poison' and I suspect

That Lancelot Andrewes and his
Committee men will get all the credit
For 'the apple of his eye' for 'a land flowing
With milk and honey' and 'the salt of the earth.'

Arrested in Antwerp and found
Guilty of heresy, you were sentenced
To be burned at the stake, and only at the last
Minute did the hangman, as an act

Of mercy, step up to tighten
The cord and garrotte you, before he lit
The fire. Oh yes, blessed are the merciful
For they shall ... How did you put it? I forget.

TO: THE RIGHT HONOURABLE THE LORD BATHURST, CIRENCESTER HALL, GLOUCESTERSHIRE

My, but they could deliver themselves
Of some wonderful one-liners, those friends
And colleagues of yours, my Lord.

                              Walpole on Kent:
'He leapt over the fence and saw that all
Nature was a garden.'

                  While Kent himself
Claimed that, 'All gardening
Is landscape painting.'

                  And I've always
Had a fondness for Sir Thomas Browne's
'Trees stand while the generations pass.'

Although that dictum proved to be very far
From the truth in your case.

                        Womaniser,
(You had seventeen children by your own wife!)
Bon viveur, wine buff, landscape gardener
And friend to Alexander Pope, you lived
To be ninety-one and so saw the trees
You'd planted in your youth not only stand
But bloom and flourish.

                        Mentioning Pope,
I do think it was a little unkind
Of you to threaten that if he didn't
Deign to visit you in Cirencester
You'd send one of your wood-carts round
To carry off his whole house and garden

And plant it down in the middle
Of Oakley Wood, where, you said,
If your children chanced upon it
While out there in the Nutting Season
They'd think it was something that you'd made
Simply to amuse them.

                     But at Twickenham,
Besides his Grotto, as you were well aware,
Pope had a vineyard, an orchard,
Grew pineapples in his hothouse,
Kept bees and had a bowling green.

He was himself 'the genius of the place',
Packing more into his five acres
Than you did into your five thousand.

And when he put down his trowel
To pick up his pen, only think
What he could pack into a couplet.

His epitaph on that young couple
Struck dead by lightning – you remember that?

Here lye two poor Lovers, who had the mishap,
Tho very chaste People, to die of a Clap.

You have to love the man.

And to have *been* loved
By Pope, as I know you were,
Must have far outweighed
Whatever fame your gardens brought you.

And I know why he loved you.
In a letter to Lady Suffolk
You wrote that the four most desirable
Things on earth were:

> old wood to burn
> old wine to drink
> old friends to converse with
> and old books to read.

Yes, Pope and I would go along with that.

TO: MR JOSEPH CORNELL, 3708 UTOPIA PARKWAY, FLUSHING, QUEENS, NEW YORK

Those tiny, perfectly interlocking
Dovetail joints (and so many of them) would,
I know, be absolutely beyond me;

But even if I did manage to make
One of your glass-fronted, wooden boxes,
There'd still be the problem of what to put

Inside it. On my kitchen windowsill
I have a stone-age scraper, a pair
Of *Cuthbert's Beads*, besides a desert rose

And seashells of various sorts and size.
But it's not the same. I chose them. There isn't
That element of serendipity

There would be if they'd offered themselves up,
Randomly. And yet, rummaging about
In the junk-shops of Queens (and there still were

Junk-shops then) you'd no option but choose, had you?
And that I suppose is where the art lies:
Your knowing the way one thing can be laid

Alongside one other thing so that
Neither will ever be the same again;
The most unremarkable of things even:

Like your four or five pale grey feathers
And a coiled spring: emblems emptied
Of explanation. It puts me in mind

Of a student demanding of me once:
Does every story have to have a meaning?
I backed off, but have often found myself

Thinking since how different our world would be
If every meaning could make our acquaintance
Accompanied already by its very own story.

TO: ANTONIO VIVALDI, OSPEDALE DELLA PIETÀ, VENICE

I've long had it in mind to write to you
About the trip we made to Venice
Earlier last year, of how quite by chance
We came across San Giovanni in Bragora,
That doleful little church you were christened in.

Then I'd meant to go on to say a few words
About the way your *Four Seasons* have been
Brutalised by Call Centres. Instead though,
I want to share with you something
I've just read: Marconi – the name means

Nothing to you, I know, but bear with me –
Marconi had come to believe that no sound,
Not one single sound ever dies completely,
But fades into the infinitesimally
Faint, the way starlight does. So I wondered,

What if, when a sound gets to the end of whatever,
It were to come bouncing back at us,
Like an echo, but an echo that comes
Gathering up its decibels again
On the way? What then would we not hear?

The dawn chorus of the pterodactyls?
Krakatoa drowning out the songs
And lamentations of lost languages,
Their airs played on instruments, the names
Of which you and I could only guess at.

If we were lucky we might just catch the end
Of the Sermon on the Mount, or those
Explosive opening chords of your *Gloria*.
But mostly, I suspect, it would be feral
Howlings and the vain harrumphings

Of politicos. And amid it all,
Coming to us from the narrow streets
Of a fetid and forgotten city,
The cry, 'Bring out your dead!', followed by
The fall of buildings and crackle of fire.

But if you'd the choice – come on, Antonio,
Play this game with me – which one sound would
You choose to hear out of all this cacophony?
Me? I'd opt for Wordsworth, as he sat
On that 'straggling heap of unhewn stones'

Reading *Michael* out loud to Coleridge.
But all this would soon get wiped out by more
Recent sounds: The Somme, Treblinka, Nagasaki,
Even the hushed and smothering snow that fell
So softly down over Stalin's gulags.

Oh, listen, quickly now, listen before it engulfs
Us all, listen with me to the rattle and clatter
Of that pert cock blackbird out there on our garden fence,
Warning its gormless young of the ominous
Pad-padding nearness of next-door's ginger cat.

TO: MENEER JAN VERMEER, OUDE LANGENDYK, DELFT

Sometimes, I like to picture myself
Striding in through the gates of Delft
So as to bring you this letter by hand –

To see the sunlight falling like a
Scatter of bright coins onto the waters
Of the canal; and behind the laughter

And chaffering of the market-place
To hear the whoosh and creak of windmills.
But that's as far as ever I'd dare go.

I wouldn't want to risk disturbing you
With irrelevant and intrusive,
Not to say impertinent questions:

*What's he just said to her, that soldier – he's turned
His back on us – to make the young girl's face
Light up that way? And the other one –*

*The one in blue – she's pregnant, isn't she?
There's good news, I trust, in the letter she's reading?*
But this, as Stevens said, is the world

As meditation, not narrative, and we
Would scarcely wish to be taken for voyeurs
Of such stilled moments, would we; moments

Which celebrate the intricacies of peace;
The cutting of fresh bread, the pouring of wine.
Either we are safe in the hands of God,

I seem to hear them say, or else all this
Will pass into oblivion. Or go, of course,
To pay the butcher's or the baker's bill.

TO: HERRA KETILL KETILLSON, ELDEY ISLAND, ICELAND

What went through your mind
    I wonder, that sunny
        morning in the June of 1844,

when you stamped on the egg
    of the last great auk
        and watched the yolk

go splattering over the toe of your boot?
    Not a lot, probably.
        After all, your two

companions had just clubbed
    the parent birds to death
        so it wasn't really any use.

Hundreds of thousands of them
    had toddled and wobbled about
        once on Funk Island

off the coast of Newfoundland,
    but then new money
        in New England

had need of feathers for its pillows
    and so, down into vats
        of boiling water

they went, fifty to a hundred
    at a time, and as there were
        no trees on Funk Island

other auks had to make do as fuel.
But sweet-smelling
ladies in the Hamptons

could now lay their peachy cheeks
down tranquilly in their
four-poster beds.

You were not alone in this though,
Ketill; in Pike County
Ohio, with the twentieth

century hardly yet begun, young
Master Southworth, aged fourteen,
went running back

into his house to get his gun
so he could bring down the last
passenger pigeon.

James Audubon – no arguing with that
authority – travelling to
Kentucky, recorded one flock

so vast it took three days to pass.
One billion was his estimate,
and that is one million

flying over you one thousand times.
But a fat young squab
served up with salt pork,

chestnut stuffing and gravy
    made for a good meal.
        And America ate them.

And then there were the macaws
    in the Amazon, the painted
        vulture and the honey creeper . . .

I write this to you looking out
    at the bird-feeder
        hanging in our garden.

True, it was a hard winter, which may
    have accounted for the wrens,
        but where have all

the finches gone, and the robins?
    Once there were blackbirds
        enough for half a singing pie.

Now we're down to three and I
    find myself smiling
        with pleasure, whenever

out from under the camellia
    our resident hedge sparrow
        creeps.

TO: DR EDWARD JENNER, THE CHANTRY, BERKELEY, GLOUCESTERSHIRE

Holidaying in the Cotswolds, we called in
At your house, a Museum to you now.
Peggy, being a biologist,
Wanted to follow the vaccination story,
But it was the Natural History Room
That held me.
                                        I'd no idea that you
Were the first person ever to witness
A blind and naked cuckoo chick heave
And hoist the other fledglings up and out
Over the side of the nest so as
To have it all to itself.
                                        (I can't remember
When I last even heard a cuckoo.)
                                                    I did like
The sound of your mentor, John Hunter, though.
Having had a giraffe from London Zoo
Stuffed for him, then finding it was too tall
To get it into his house in Jermyn Street,
He chopped its legs off just below the knee
So it could then stand in his hallway
To greet his visitors.

                                        Anatomist,
Surgeon and polymath, 'I love to be puzzled,'
He once said, 'for then I am sure
To learn something valuable.'
And in reply to your questions he gave you
Words of advice you never forgot: 'Why think
About it? Try the experiment.'
                                        And you did.
You drowned a swallow to prove they never could,
As some believed, hibernate under water.

And you vaccinated little James Phipps,
Then quite deliberately gave him smallpox.

Smallpox: such a democratic disease,
Wiping out the Incas and the Aztecs
And at least six of the crowned heads of Europe.

It's strange, isn't it, that the first symptom
Wasn't physical at all, but an
Unexplained feeling of anxiety,
As though the body knew already
What was in store for it.

                    First the fever,
The convulsions, the stabbing pains, the rash
And then the blisters, which spread until the whole skin
Looked as black as if it had been roasted,
And slid off the body in sheets. And the stench.
'Turning the babe into a changeling
At which the mother shuddered, and making
The eyes and cheeks of the beloved maiden
Objects of horror to her lover.'

But Sarah Nelmes, a milkmaid, told you
That girls who caught cowpox never got smallpox.

So why think about it? Why not try
The experiment? There was Blossom the cow
And there was young James Phipps,
So you took a hold of his little arm . . .

But what I always wonder, and have to ask
Is: were you really that confident?
Really? Because, you know, if you weren't . . .
No, perhaps it's better not to ask.

TO: MR ALEXANDER SELKIRK, LOWER LARGO, FIFE

A good agent, that's what you needed,
Someone who could have stopped Defoe
Stealing your story. After all, it wasn't long
Before all the ballad-mongers were singing:

> *Robinson Crusoe, rumour is rife,*
> *Was born in Lower Largo, Fife.*

A shoemaker's son, and a seventh son
To boot (if you'll pardon the pun). Not
That it brought you any luck. No, I'd say
You put paid to that old myth.

                 Quarrelsome,
And moody, you were at loggerheads
With almost everyone you sailed with,
Until Juan Fernandez, where they dumped you
Ashore with a pistol, some bullets,
A Bible, a hatchet, a flask of rum,
Two pounds of tobacco and a kettle.

Crusoe of course had it made from the start.
Not only was he the sole survivor
Of a shipwreck, the vessel then drifted in
So close to land he got enough stuff off
To set up his own ship's chandlers.

                And what
A prig that man was, and what a bore. On
And on he goes, listing his achievements.
You know, Sandy, he even re-invented
The umbrella. It took him all of two
Sentences.

Which reminds me – where did he
Get all the ink for that interminable journal?
Gradually, it seems, you lost the habit
Of speech. But even talking to yourself
There'd be words you had no need of – words like
Neighbourliness for one, and *unpunctual*,
Or *pillowcase*.

But getting back to Crusoe,
Friday. Man Friday. Clearly he wasn't
Entitled to a Christian name. 'And thou
Mayst call me *Master*.' That says it all.

You lived alone there for over four years,
Alone but for the rats that came gnawing
At your feet in the night, and the cats you tamed
To kill those rats, and the toothsome goats of course.

The reality of it all is more
Than we can guess at. To live alone
A man must be either a beast or a god,
Said Aristotle, yet Thoreau declared
That he had never found a companion
So companionable as solitude.

Your predicament Roy Plomley turned
Into a radio parlour game: eight records,
One luxury item, and a book – apart
From the Bible and Shakespeare.
Well, I know which one I won't be taking.

TO: THE GOD, MERCURY, MT. OLYMPUS, GREECE

(Indebted somewhat to Horace, *Odes* 1.10)

Bright Lord of Eloquence, grandchild
Of our round world's upholder, we chased
Quick globules of you across the deep-grained
Bench-tops in our grammar school,
Unaware then that grammar had been
Your sometime gift to gaping man
Squatted in his cave mouth. Yes,
Mercury, it is to you I sing, messenger
To Jupiter, figurehead of Interflora
And bringer of packages from Amazon.

Liar, and inventor of the stringed lyre,
Joker too: only two days old when you rustled
Apollo's cattle, but he could only laugh;
No point in getting angry
When you'd filched his arrows too.

Later and kindlier, you led grieving Priam
Through the dark lines of the Greek camp
To urge the iron-hearted, man-slaying Achilles
That he might come to terms over the burial
Of Hector, Tamer of Horses.

Multi- talented – *Psychopomp* (a rather
Ugly word) they wrote on the job-spec
Granting you the guidance of lost souls
Down to Lethe and the Styx. Summoned
By your golden wand one day, we will
Of course go with you, but would
That our passage thither might,
I pray thee good my Lord,
Prove to be both easeful and benign.

TO: MR HENRY JAMES, DUNWICH, SUFFOLK

If challenged, one would, and on this, I believe, we should in all likelihood, find ourselves in close agreement, feel obliged, albeit reluctantly, to admit that travelling so very far, and so very incommodiously, to a place self-evidently, and famously, no longer there, could, by some, be construed as rather perverse, yet the mind which can, as you put it, 'properly brood', might manage to ignore the vastness of the car park and the dreadful Café {Two *Sludgeatas* and a *Depresso* coming up!} and re-populate this city, which now consists of little more than the letters of its name, desolate and exquisite *Dunwich*, but which blossomed once between the bounty of the land and the bounteous but bludgeoning sea; we might, as I say, populate it once again with mariners and merchants, shoemakers and chandlers, housewives and fishwives, and re-build for them their windmills and workshops, their chapels and taverns, churches and hovels, and hear, even as we are preparing to depart, the bells ring out their carillon beneath the waves; any counter-argument to any of this, based on mere matter of fact, being, as we both know, of singularly little relevance, if indeed of any.

TO: DAME FREYA STARK, CASA FREIA, ASOLO, VENETO, ITALY

I slid my damp tray
along the shiny metal rails,
ordered a small latte,
picked up a cinnamon muffin
and brought it over here
to a table by the window
where I could watch the traffic on the M6.

Nobody was talking.
Muzak betrayed the silence.
We might have been painted by Edward Hopper.
And it was only when looking out
for the Eddie Stobarts
and Norbert Dentressangles
had begun to pall
that I opened your *Journey's Echo*.

And by page two there you were
sailing among the islands
in the Ionian Sea.
It was twilight.
You asked the name
of one you could see
drifting away into the west
and 'Ithaca, the captain said,
as if the name were mere geography.'
Ithaca.

In the deserts of Syria
it was 'as if one were suddenly
in the very morning of the world,
among the people of Abraham and Jacob.'

Sayyid, the watchmaker, told you
there were five reasons for travel:
> to leave one's troubles behind one
> to earn a living
> to acquire learning
> to practise good manners
> and to meet honourable men

Sight-seeing and soaking up the rays
never entered his head.

You were, as someone said,
the last of the Romantic Travellers.
Travelling with the Bedouin to Damascus
you delighted in the grace
and fluidity of the camels;
lived in harems,
dined with pashas and emirs
fell prey to malaria and dysentery.

Baudelaire once wrote:
> *We saw stars,*
> *And waves; we saw sand too*
> *And despite many crises and unforeseen disasters,*
> *We were often bored, just as we are here.*

Surprise
is hard to come by now.
Guide books tell us not only
what to see, but how to see it.

And the brochures:
Petra and The Alhambra;

and that sun-bleached cove
with its palm trees leaning out,
always at the same angle
under an impossibly indigo sky.

Hardship
is the immigration line
at O'Hare.

My coffee must be getting cold by now,
that's your fault, Freya.
And I haven't even touched my muffin.
Reproachful, it squats there
in its paper shroud
like some shrivelled sepia cauliflower.

Well, it's about time
I took my leave
of this oasis
and got back among the Norberts.

By four
I should have made it as far south
down the M5 as *Michael Wood*;
that's if I'm lucky.

TO: ODYSSEUS, ON THE ISLAND OF CALYPSO

Once the waves had done nudging and
Shoving you, half dead, up over the shingle,
And you came to, and found her
Standing there, smiling at you like something

Out of *Victoria's Secret*,
You must have thought you'd died and gone to heaven.
Truth to tell though, I'm not sure
What your own views were on the after-life.

For one thing, you'd been there yourself
And seen it, that time you went looking
For Tiresias. You very nearly turned
Green with fear then, so they say,

As the sheeted dead came crawling
Out of Erebus, thirsting after the blood
Of your sacrifice, and you keeping your own mother
Back from it with your drawn sword!

But let's get back to Calypso.
(And by the by, her name should have warned you:
It means *Deceit*.) But she was, Oh
So fragrant, wasn't she, as she washed your wounds

And tended to your each and every
Need. As fragrant she was as the jasmine
And lilac that lined the garden path
She led you up. Man, but it took you long enough

To realise no rain, no leaf
No petal ever fell there: every thing everywhere
Perfection; each day dawning
A perfect replica of the one before,

Until it began to irritate,
And then to irritate into an itch
For autumn. So now here you are
Slouching up and down the beach again

Counting the ever-changing waves,
Your thoughts weaving their way over the wide
Waters back home to Ithaca,
And to Penelope. She'd be – what – in her

Forties now? And even at her
Best not much of a looker, but still you
Miss her, don't you? Well, don't despair.
Zeus has it all in hand. I know.

I've read the story. It won't ever
Be plain sailing of course. You've forgotten
What domesticity is like:
Fights with the neighbours and silly quarrels

Over furniture. In time though
You'll find yourself sitting by the fireside
With tales of your own to tell,
And trying to explain to your children's

Children, if they'd but listen, that there is
Much to be said for mortality.

TO: HORACE, THE SABINE FARM, NR. TIVOLI

Let me be quite clear: I would no more claim
Comparison with you than a sparrow – albeit
Both birds – would with an osprey;
Though it amuses me to think we do
Share a certain kinship in that we both
Set out as soldiers and civil servants.

I spent my National Service at a NATO
Headquarters in Fontainebleau, which, truth to tell,
Was something of an idyllic doddle,
Whereas you (why, I can not understand)
Fought alongside Brutus at the Battle
Of Philippi. And what a fiasco
That was. 'Thou shalt see me at Philippi,'
The stately ghost of Caesar declared
Unto him. Not one word of that ever leaked down
Through the ranks to you lot though, I'll bet.

                                                Wisely,
You had the good sense not to stay and fall
On your sword 'in the high Roman fashion'.
You ran.

        They made you pay for it though:
They commandeered your family's farm. But you
Got a job as a clerk in the treasury
And clawed your way back into favour.
                               Me?
I was in Whitehall, the Air Ministry –
Work I quite liked, but before long I had
Begun to loathe London.

And it's here
Our two paths – not to mention our talents –
Diverge. You had that lucky break. You met
Virgil (you know I sometimes find it hard
To believe he was real – something to do
With Dante I suspect) and through him
Your patron Maecenas. Patrons, sadly,
Had become extinct long before my time.

Then came your poems.

One thing I do know
Is that we both liked to write on the hoof.
A small Moleskin Notebook and a pencil
Come with me most places I go. You
Must have had to hold lines in your head,
The way Wordsworth did, until you got home
To your stylus.

Two words you wrote
Set off such ripples as you never could
Have imagined: *Beatus ille.* Yes,
Happy the man who had the luck to live
Simply and contentedly in that
Rural retreat you painted for us,
Our own personalised Eden.

From that moment
It seemed to be every poet's
Abiding obsession – from Andrew Marvell's
'Green thoughts in a green shade' to Yeats's
Own *Isle of Innisfree.*

Some even made it.
I'm thinking here of the Grotto Pope dug
Under his house in Twickenham and decorated
With stalactites shot down from the walls
Of Wookey Hole with a blunderbuss!

In our own day, Elizabeth Bishop
(You'd like her poems, I feel sure) found
Her 'dream house' while out walking along by the sea,
And imagined herself living there, doing
Nothing, or nothing much; looking out
Through binoculars; talking to herself;
Reading long boring books and writing down
Useless notes. In fact, being a poet.

For her, of course, it was a dream; she knew that.
But Maecenas gave you the thing itself –
A farm a mile or so beyond Varia
On a slight rise above the river;
So easy to picture now from the way
You describe it: how it catches the early
Morning sun and is then warmed by it again
Of an evening; its orchards, olive groves,
And vineyards; plum trees and wild cherry.
From your villa with its pillared courtyard
Open to the sky, you had a clear view
Out across the valley and could hear the soft
Sounds of running water.

                It was there you wrote
Your *Letters*. Small wonder then that they
Sound so relaxed. Your aim, you once said,
Was to write about familiar things

In a verse which looked as if nothing
Could be easier – even though it cost
A deal of sweat to do it; and so make
Something which was quite wonderful out of
'Noting much'.

                    Our garden, you might say,
Is nothing much – smaller than your villa
Certainly, but we have honeysuckle,
Roses and sweet peas, and a path that winds
All of fourteen paces between blue
And grey slate chippings. Even a small pond.
And a dozen or more pots that Peggy
Has planted out with hosta, begonias
And geranium.
                    And it is here now
That I am sitting, finishing this letter,
Watching the leaves of an oak tree
That isn't even ours come cluttering down
All around me.
                    Just one more thing.
                                        I want
You to understand that of all the people
I've written to, it is you I would most like
To hear back from.
                    Yes, even in Latin.

Sed nos immensum spatiis confecimus aequor,
et iam tempus equum fumantia solvere colla.

VIRGIL